Illinois
Bingo Book

A COMPLETE BINGO GAME IN A BOOK

ILLINOIS

Written By Rebecca Stark

ISBN 978-0-87386-506-7

Educational Books 'n' Bingo

Printed in the U.S.A.

DIRECTIONS

INCLUDED:

List of Terms

Templates for Additional Terms and Clues

2 Clues per Term

30 Unique Bingo Cards

Markers

1. **Either cut apart the book or make copies of ALL the sheets. You might want to make an extra copy of the clue sheets to use for introduction and review. Keep the sheets in an envelope for easy reuse.**

2. Cut apart the call cards with terms and clues.

3. Pass out one bingo card per student. There are enough for a class of 30.

4. Pass out markers. You may cut apart the markers included in this book or use any other small items of your choice.

5. Decide whether or not you will require the entire card to be filled. Requiring the entire card to be filled provides a better review. However, if you have a short time to fill, you may prefer to have them do the just the border or some other format. Tell the class before you begin what is required.

6. There are 50 terms. Read the list before you begin. If there are any terms that have not been covered in class, you may want to read to the students the term and clues before you begin.

7. There is a blank space in the middle of each card. You can instruct the students to use it as a free space or you can write in answers to cover terms not included. Of course, in this case you would create your own clues. (Templates provided.)

8. Shuffle the cards and place them in a pile. Two or three clues are provided for each term. If you plan to play the game with the same group more than once, you might want to choose a different clue for each game. If not, you may choose to use more than one clue.

9. Be sure to keep the cards you have used for the present game in a separate pile. When a student calls, "Bingo," he or she will have to verify that the correct answers are on his or her card AND that the markers were placed in response to the proper questions. Pull out the cards that are on the student's card keeping them in the order they were used in the game. Read each clue as it was given and ask the student to identify the correct answer from his or her card.

10. If the student has the correct answers on the card AND has shown that they were marked in response to the *correct questions,* then that student is the winner and the game is over. If the student does not have the correct answers on the card OR he or she marked the answers in response to *the wrong questions,* then the game continues until there is a proper winner.

11. If you want to play again, reshuffle the cards and begin again.

Have fun!

TERMS INCLUDED

Apple(s)

Aurora

Big Bluestem

Black Hawk

Bluegill

Border

Capital

Cardinal(s)

Central Lowland

Charles Mound

Chicago

Chicago Fire

Civil War

Climate

Corn

Crop(s)

County (-ies)

Eastern Tiger Salamander(s)

Executive Branch

Flag

Flourite

Galena

Gulf Coastal

James Butler Hickok

Illini

Illinois Territory

Industry (-ies)

Judicial Branch

Lake Michigan

Legislative Branch

Lincoln

Marquette and Joliet

Mines (-ed)

Mississippi River

Monarch Butterfly

Barack Obama

Painted Turtle

Prairie

River(s)

Rockford

Ronald Reagan

Seal

Shawnee Hills

Song

Springfield

Tully Monster

Union

Flourite

Charles Rudolph Walgreen

White Oak

Wrigley Field

Additional Terms

Choose as many additional terms as you would like and write them in the squares. Repeat each as desired.
Cut out the squares and randomly distribute them to the class.
Instruct the students to place their square on the center space of their card.

Illinois Bingo

Clues for Additional Terms

Write three clues for each of your additional terms.

1. _____ 2. 3.	1. _____ 2. 3.
1. _____ 2. 3.	1. _____ 2. 3.
1. _____ 2. 3.	1. _____ 2. 3.

Illinois Bingo

ILLINOIS ILLINOIS ILLINOIS ILLINOIS ILLINOIS

ILLINOIS ILLINOIS ILLINOIS ILLINOIS ILLINOIS

ILLINOIS ILLINOIS ILLINOIS ILLINOIS ILLINOIS

ILLINOIS ILLINOIS ILLINOIS ILLINOIS ILLINOIS

ILLINOIS ILLINOIS ILLINOIS ILLINOIS ILLINOIS

ILLINOIS ILLINOIS ILLINOIS ILLINOIS ILLINOIS

ILLINOIS ILLINOIS ILLINOIS ILLINOIS ILLINOIS

Apple(s) 1. The state fruit is the gold rush ___. 2. ___ are the most important fruit crop.	**Aurora** 1. It is the second largest city in the state. The historic downtown area of ___ is centered on Stolp Island. 2. ___ is nicknamed "City of Lights" because it was one of the first cities to have an all-electric street-lighting system.
Big Bluestem 1. ___ is the official state grass of Illinois. 2. ___ is sometimes called Prairie tallgrass.	**Black Hawk** 1. ___ was a Sauk warrior. During the War of 1812, he fought on the side of the British. He later led a band of Sauk during the brief conflict known as the ___ War. 2. After the ___War, the Sauk had to cede the land west of the Mississippi River to the United States. This opened the land to white settlement.
Bluegill 1. The ___ is the official state fish. 2. This freshwater fish is a member of the sunfish family. It has a black spot behind its gills.	**Border** 1. These states ___ Illinois: Wisconsin, Kentucky, Illinois, Indiana, Iowa and Missouri. 2. Lake Michigan forms part of the state's eastern ___.
Capital 1. Kaskaskia was the first ___ of the state of Illinois, followed by Vandalia. 2. Springfield became the ___ of the state of Illinois in 1837.	**Cardinal(s)** 1. The state bird is the ___. 2. Male ___ are a brilliant scarlet red; females are a buffy brown with reddish wings.
Central Lowland 1. The ___ covers about 90% of the state. It extends over all but the most southern part of the state. 2. The ___ Region can be sub-divided into the Great Lakes Plain, the Driftless Plains and the Till Plains. The Till Plains are typical of the flat farmlands of Illinois. Illinois Bingo	**Charles Mound** 1. At 1,235 feet, ___ is the highest natural point in the state. 2. ___, the highest natural point in Illinois, is near the small town of Scales Mound, about 11 miles northeast of Galena. It is on privately owned farmland. © Barbara M. Peller

Chicago

1. The ___ Metropolitan Area is the 3rd largest metropolitan area in the nation.
2. ___ has many nicknames. Among them are "Windy City," "Second City," and the "The White City."

Chicago Fire

1. Legend says that the ___ of 1871 started in the barn of Mr. and Mrs. Patrick and Catherine O'Leary, but the actual cause is unknown.
2. Whatever the cause, several factors influenced the spread of the ___ : the city's overuse of wood for building, a drought, and strong winds.

Civil War

1. No ___ battles were fought in the state.
2. Most Illinoisans supported the Union during the ___, and Illinois was an important source of troops for the Union army.

Climate

1. The ___ of Illinois is characterized by warm to hot summers and cool to cold winters.
2. The ___ of Chicago and other areas along the shores of Lake Michigan is affected by their nearness to the lake.

Corn

1. ___ is grown throughout the state and occupies two-fifths of all cropland. Pop___ is the state snack food.
2. The ___ Belt is a major agricultural region of the MIdwest. It is centered in Iowa and Illinois.

Crop(s)

1. Corn, soybeans, hay, wheat, rye, oats, and grain sorghum are important ___.
2. Corn and soybeans are the most important ___.

County (-ies)

1. There are 102 ___ in Illinois. Chicago is in Cook ___.
2. Cook ___ is the most populous in Illinois and the second most populous in the nation after Los Angeles ___.

Eastern Tiger Salamander(s)

1. The ___ is the state amphibian.
2. The body color of this amphibian is dark brown with irregular blotches of yellow or olive.

Executive Branch

1. The ___ comprises the governor, lieutenant governor, secretary of state, comptroller, attorney general, and various departments.
2. The governor is the head of the ___. The present-day governor is [fill in].

Flag

1. The state ___ has a representation of the state seal centered on a white field.
2. Beneath the seal on the state ___ is the word "ILLINOIS."

Illinois Bingo

© Barbara M. Peller

Flourite
1. ___ is the state mineral. Illinois is the largest producer of this mineral in the United States.
2. The name ___ comes from the Latin *fluere,* which means "to flow." It comes from the fact that this mineral melts easily.

Galena
1. The city of ___ is known for its history and historical architecture. The home of Ulysses S. Grant is in this city.
2. The city ___ is named for the mineral, which is the natural form of lead sulfide and the most important lead ore mineral.

Gulf Coastal
1. The flat alluvial lands of the ___ Plain cover extreme southern part of the state.
2. The ___ Plain is south of the Shawnee Hills.
(*alluvial* = related to soil material, such as clay, silt, sand, or gravel, deposited by running water)

James Butler Hickok
1. ___ was born in Troy Grove, Illinois. He is better known as "Wild Bill."
2. This gunfighter, scout, and lawman was a folk hero of the American Old West.

Illini
1. These Algonquin-speaking Native Americans were allies of the French fur traders and colonists.
2. The most populous tribes of the ___ Confederation were the Kaskaskia, the Cahokia, the Peoria, the Tamaroa, and the Michigamea. The Iroquois were their enemies.

Illinois Territory
1. The ___ was created by the Northwest Ordinance of 1787. It existed from March 1, 1809, until December 3, 1818.
2. A large portion of the ___ included what is now the state of Illinois. It also included parts of Michigan, Minnesota and Wisconsin. When Illinois became a state, the ___ ceased to exist.

Industry (-ies)
1. The production of industrial machinery is the most important manufacturing ___. Food processing, printing and publishing, fishing, chemicals, and manufacturing are also important.
2. Agriculture and mining are important

___ .

Judicial Branch
1. The ___ interprets what our laws mean and makes decisions about the laws and those who break them.
2. It is made up of several courts, the highest of which is the state Supreme Court.

Lake Michigan
1. ___ is one of the five Great Lakes of North America; it is the only one located entirely within the United States.
2. Chicago, a major port city, is on the southwestern shore of ___ .

Legislative Branch
1. The state ___, called the General Assembly, consists of a Senate and a House of Representatives.
2. The ___ makes the laws.

Lincoln
1. The state slogan is Land of ___. His image and the slogan are on the state quarter.
2. He was the 16th President of the United States. Although not born in Illinois, he began his political career in the state.

Marquette and Joliet
1. This team comprised a Jesuit missionary and a fur trader.
2. They explored the unsettled territory from the Great Lakes region to the Gulf of Mexico for France.

Mines (-ed)
1. Coal, crushed stone, and oil are the most valuable ___ products in Illinois.
2. Coal has been ___ in 73 counties in Illinois. Most coal ___ in Illinois are underground.

Mississippi River
1. The ___ is the chief river of the largest river system in North America. It flows for about 450 miles from the northern border of the state to its southern tip.
2. The Illinois River and the Ohio River are both tributaries of the ___.

Monarch Butterfly
1. The state insect is the ___.
2. Both the caterpillar and the adult ___ are   brilliant in color as a warning to predators that it is poisonous.

Barack Obama
1. ___ became the 44th President of the United States on January 20, 2009.
2. ___ was United States senator from Illinois before becoming President of the United States.

Painted Turtle
1. The ___ is the state reptile.
2. This reptile is so-named because of the yellow, red, and orange markings on the head, shell, and underside.

Prairie
1. The ___ State is an unofficial state nick-name. Each year the 3rd full week in September is observed as Illinois ___ Week.
2. A ___ is level or rolling land with deep, fertile soil; a cover of tall coarse grasses; and few trees. Most of the state was once covered with ___ grasses.

River(s)
1. The Illinois, the Mississippi, the Ohio, and the Wabash are ___ in Illinois.
2. The Illinois ___ is a principal tributary of the Mississippi ___. Its watershed is the most important in the state.

Rockford
1. ___ is sometimes called "The Forest City" because of its elm trees.
2. This city along the Rock River is the county seat of Winnebago County.

Illinois Bingo

Ronald Reagan 1. ___ was born in Tampico, Illinois. 2. ___ was the 40th President of the United States.	**Seal** 1. The Great ___ features a bald eagle on a rock; it has a shield in its talons and a banner with the state motto in its beak. 2. The state motto, "State sovereignty, national union," is part of the Great ___.
Shawnee Hills 1. The ___ region is the name for the Illinois Ozarks. Shawnee National Forest and Lusk Creek Canyon are in this region. 2. The ___ region is south of the Central Lowland. Sandstone canyons are one of the outstanding features of this scenic area.	**Song** 1. The state ___ is "Illinois." 2. The state ___ begins, "By thy rivers gently flowing."
Springfield 1. ___ is the third and present capital of Illinois. 2. The Lincoln Home National Historic Site is in ___, Illinois.	**Tully Monster** 1. The ___ is the official state fossil. Its formal name is *Tullimonstrum gregarium.* 2. The extinct ___ was a soft-bodied animal that lived in the ocean that covered much of Illinois about 300 million years ago.
Union 1. Illinois was admitted to the ___ on December 3, 1818. 2. When Illinois joined the ___, it became the 21st state.	**Charles Rudolph Walgreen** 1. This businessman was born in Knoxville, Illinois. By 1927, ___ had established 110 drug stores. 2. His chain of stores introduced the first malted milk shake in 1922.
White Oak 1. The ___ is the state tree. 2. The ___ is important because its acorns are an important source of food for wildlife when their food is scarce.	**Wrigley Field** 1. The Chicago Cubs play at ___. 2. In 1926 Cubs Park was changed to ___ after the chewing-gum magnet who bought the team.

Illinois Bingo

Illinois Bingo

River(s)	Apple(s)	Big Bluestem	Executive Branch	Bluegill
County (-ies)	Aurora	Charles Rudolph Walgreen	Lincoln	Seal
Flourite	Legislative Branch		Barack Obama	White Oak
Union	Ronald Reagan	Tully Monster	Lake Michigan	Mines (-ed)
Monarch Butterfly	Gulf Coastal	Climate	Song	Illinois Territory

Illinois Bingo: Card No. 1

Illinois Bingo

Union	Flourite	Illini	Rockford	Judicial Branch
Mines (-ed)	Corn	Cardinal(s)	Ronald Reagan	Mississippi River
Charles Mound	Gulf Coastal		James Butler Hickok	Tully Monster
Painted Turtle	Prairie	Legislative Branch	Wrigley Field	Bluegill
Seal	Charles Rudolph Walgreen	Climate	County (-ies)	Song

Illinois Bingo

Gulf Coastal	Tully Monster	Corn	Lake Michigan	Flourite
Mines (-ed)	Aurora	Central Lowland	Apple(s)	Galena
Ronald Reagan	Charles Rudolph Walgreen		Mississippi River	Black Hawk
Legislative Branch	Charles Mound	Monarch Butterfly	Painted Turtle	Illini
Song	Chicago	Climate	Wrigley Field	Judicial Branch

Illinois Bingo

Legislative Branch	Mississippi River	Big Bluestem	Chicago	Judicial Branch
Marquette and Joliet	Capital	Apple(s)	Rockford	Flourite
Barack Obama	Painted Turtle		Illinois Territory	Executive Branch
Tully Monster	Aurora	Charles Rudolph Walgreen	Climate	Cardinal(s)
Chicago Fire	Seal	Border	Song	White Oak

Illinois Bingo: Card No. 4

Illinois Bingo

Seal	Bluegill	Ronald Reagan	Cardinal(s)	Chicago
Marquette and Joliet	Tully Monster	Central Lowland	James Butler Hickok	Aurora
Big Bluestem	White Oak		Lincoln	Flag
Illinois Territory	Judicial Branch	River(s)	Wrigley Field	Civil War
Corn	Climate	Flourite	Legislative Branch	Barack Obama

Illinois Bingo: Card No. 5

Illinois Bingo

Black Hawk	Mississippi River	Illini	Judicial Branch	White Oak
Lake Michigan	Ronald Reagan	Civil War	Apple(s)	Flourite
Rockford	Chicago Fire		Capital	James Butler Hickok
Climate	Monarch Butterfly	Wrigley Field	Border	Big Bluestem
Mines (-ed)	Cardinal(s)	River(s)	Barack Obama	Crop(s)

Illinois Bingo

River(s)	Mississippi River	Flag	Tully Monster	Corn
Mines (-ed)	Judicial Branch	Gulf Coastal	Aurora	Marquette and Joliet
White Oak	Executive Branch		James Butler Hickok	Capital
Legislative Branch	Painted Turtle	Central Lowland	Union	Charles Mound
Climate	Chicago	Wrigley Field	Border	Black Hawk

Illinois Bingo: Card No. 7

Illinois Bingo

Barack Obama	Mississippi River	Eastern Tiger Salamander(s)	Lake Michigan	Capital
Marquette and Joliet	Big Bluestem	Rockford	White Oak	Cardinal(s)
Crop(s)	Chicago		Judicial Branch	Bluegill
Song	Legislative Branch	Union	Chicago Fire	Painted Turtle
Charles Rudolph Walgreen	Climate	Border	Ronald Reagan	Mines (-ed)

Illinois Bingo: Card No. 8

Illinois Bingo

James Butler Hickok	Corn	Gulf Coastal	Crop(s)	Chicago
Chicago Fire	Judicial Branch	Barack Obama	Ronald Reagan	Mississippi River
Galena	River(s)		Aurora	Eastern Tiger Salamander(s)
Civil War	Bluegill	Monarch Butterfly	Lincoln	Flag
Painted Turtle	Wrigley Field	Central Lowland	Union	Illinois Territory

Illinois Bingo: Card No. 9

Illinois Bingo

Union	Lake Michigan	Capital	Rockford	Crop(s)
White Oak	Cardinal(s)	Apple(s)	Aurora	Judicial Branch
Chicago	Mississippi River		Executive Branch	Charles Mound
Monarch Butterfly	Illinois Territory	Civil War	Wrigley Field	Galena
Central Lowland	Mines (-ed)	Illini	Seal	Barack Obama

Illinois Bingo: Card No. 10

Illinois Bingo

Black Hawk	Mississippi River	Ronald Reagan	Civil War	Mines (-ed)
Eastern Tiger Salamander(s)	Galena	Lincoln	James Butler Hickok	Apple(s)
Marquette and Joliet	Judicial Branch		Illini	Gulf Coastal
Central Lowland	Flourite	Wrigley Field	Chicago	Union
Chicago Fire	Climate	River(s)	Border	Corn

Illinois Bingo

Corn	Bluegill	Galena	Lake Michigan	James Butler Hickok
Gulf Coastal	Mines (-ed)	Big Bluestem	Border	Aurora
River(s)	Flag		White Oak	Rockford
Climate	Painted Turtle	Judicial Branch	Union	Marquette and Joliet
Mississippi River	Eastern Tiger Salamander(s)	Chicago	Chicago Fire	Cardinal(s)

Illinois Bingo: Card No. 12

Illinois Bingo

Civil War	Bluegill	Black Hawk	Galena	White Oak
Big Bluestem	Eastern Tiger Salamander(s)	Judicial Branch	James Butler Hickok	Charles Mound
Lake Michigan	Cardinal(s)		Gulf Coastal	Flag
Barack Obama	Wrigley Field	Capital	Chicago	Union
Climate	Illinois Territory	Border	River(s)	Lincoln

Illinois Bingo: Card No. 13

Illinois Bingo

County (-ies)	Judicial Branch	Ronald Reagan	James Butler Hickok	Chicago Fire
Cardinal(s)	River(s)	Galena	Aurora	Mississippi River
Civil War	Executive Branch		Illini	Central Lowland
Illinois Territory	Wrigley Field	Chicago	Capital	Black Hawk
Climate	Rockford	Charles Mound	Mines (-ed)	Barack Obama

Illinois Bingo

Lincoln	James Butler Hickok	Ronald Reagan	Corn	Lake Michigan
Black Hawk	Illini	Apple(s)	Big Bluestem	Chicago Fire
White Oak	River(s)		Flourite	Mississippi River
Climate	Galena	Eastern Tiger Salamander(s)	Wrigley Field	Civil War
Mines (-ed)	Painted Turtle	Border	Crop(s)	Gulf Coastal

Illinois Bingo

Capital	Galena	Eastern Tiger Salamander(s)	Crop(s)	Prairie
Rockford	Charles Mound	Flag	Marquette and Joliet	Executive Branch
Civil War	Bluegill		White Oak	Gulf Coastal
Legislative Branch	Cardinal(s)	Climate	Lincoln	Union
Chicago Fire	Springfield	Border	Painted Turtle	Mississippi River

Illinois Bingo

Central Lowland	Shawnee Hills	Industry (-ies)	Galena	County (-ies)
Lincoln	Chicago Fire	Wrigley Field	Executive Branch	Flag
James Butler Hickok	Barack Obama		Springfield	Eastern Tiger Salamander(s)
Illinois Territory	Mines (-ed)	Union	Ronald Reagan	Charles Mound
Monarch Butterfly	Civil War	Corn	Lake Michigan	Bluegill

Illinois Bingo

Crop(s)	Chicago	Cardinal(s)	Civil War	Rockford
Mississippi River	Central Lowland	Monarch Butterfly	White Oak	Chicago Fire
James Butler Hickok	Charles Mound		Industry (-ies)	Big Bluestem
Bluegill	Apple(s)	Wrigley Field	Union	Illini
Springfield	Galena	Ronald Reagan	Shawnee Hills	Black Hawk

Illinois Bingo

White Oak	Black Hawk	Galena	Eastern Tiger Salamander(s)	Union
Lincoln	Lake Michigan	Mississippi River	Corn	Executive Branch
Shawnee Hills	Chicago		Aurora	Flourite
Illini	Springfield	Monarch Butterfly	Painted Turtle	Industry (-ies)
Big Bluestem	Prairie	Mines (-ed)	Barack Obama	Border

Illinois Bingo: Card No. 19

Illinois Bingo

County (-ies)	Shawnee Hills	Lake Michigan	Galena	Border
Cardinal(s)	Gulf Coastal	Marquette and Joliet	Monarch Butterfly	Rockford
Bluegill	Flag		Legislative Branch	Apple(s)
Seal	Charles Rudolph Walgreen	Song	Painted Turtle	Springfield
Tully Monster	Barack Obama	Prairie	Union	Industry (-ies)

Illinois Bingo

Lincoln	Black Hawk	Marquette and Joliet	Galena	Seal
Bluegill	Industry (-ies)	Capital	Eastern Tiger Salamander(s)	River(s)
Charles Mound	Mines (-ed)		Shawnee Hills	Ronald Reagan
Monarch Butterfly	Corn	Springfield	Illinois Territory	Barack Obama
Legislative Branch	Prairie	Border	Central Lowland	Painted Turtle

Illinois Bingo: Card No. 21

Illinois Bingo

Crop(s)	Illini	Industry (-ies)	Big Bluestem	Civil War
Rockford	Lake Michigan	Flourite	Eastern Tiger Salamander(s)	Aurora
Cardinal(s)	Executive Branch		River(s)	Flag
Springfield	Illinois Territory	Painted Turtle	Apple(s)	Marquette and Joliet
Prairie	Central Lowland	Shawnee Hills	Charles Mound	Legislative Branch

Illinois Bingo: Card No. 22

Illinois Bingo

Capital	Shawnee Hills	Corn	Big Bluestem	Border
Black Hawk	County (-ies)	Mines (-ed)	Lincoln	Apple(s)
Illini	Civil War		Song	River(s)
Charles Mound	Prairie	Springfield	Central Lowland	Painted Turtle
Seal	Charles Rudolph Walgreen	Barack Obama	Monarch Butterfly	Industry (-ies)

Illinois Bingo

Capital	Barack Obama	County (-ies)	Shawnee Hills	Eastern Tiger Salamander(s)
Industry (-ies)	Border	Marquette and Joliet	Rockford	River(s)
Flag	Crop(s)		Civil War	Charles Mound
Seal	Song	Springfield	Central Lowland	Bluegill
Tully Monster	Legislative Branch	Prairie	Lake Michigan	Charles Rudolph Walgreen

Illinois Bingo: Card No. 24

Illinois Bingo

Legislative Branch	Marquette and Joliet	Shawnee Hills	Ronald Reagan	Industry (-ies)
Apple(s)	Bluegill	Lincoln	Capital	Aurora
Illinois Territory	Eastern Tiger Salamander(s)		Song	Springfield
Flourite	Seal	Charles Rudolph Walgreen	Prairie	Executive Branch
Border	County (-ies)	Cardinal(s)	Chicago Fire	Tully Monster

Illinois Bingo

Industry (-ies)	Shawnee Hills	Illini	Rockford	Crop(s)
Monarch Butterfly	Lake Michigan	Eastern Tiger Salamander(s)	County (-ies)	Capital
Illinois Territory	Song		Executive Branch	Legislative Branch
Central Lowland	Big Bluestem	Seal	Prairie	Springfield
Flag	Chicago Fire	Ronald Reagan	Charles Rudolph Walgreen	Tully Monster

Illinois Bingo

Illini	Cardinal(s)	Shawnee Hills	County (-ies)	Gulf Coastal
Seal	Song	Lincoln	Springfield	Aurora
Wrigley Field	Charles Rudolph Walgreen		Prairie	Legislative Branch
Crop(s)	Black Hawk	Marquette and Joliet	Tully Monster	Apple(s)
Chicago Fire	Executive Branch	Industry (-ies)	Flourite	Flag

Illinois Bingo

Illini	County (-ies)	Flourite	Shawnee Hills	Capital
Gulf Coastal	Industry (-ies)	Song	Rockford	Executive Branch
Charles Rudolph Walgreen	Charles Mound		Flag	Monarch Butterfly
Union	Crop(s)	Mines (-ed)	Prairie	Springfield
Big Bluestem	James Butler Hickok	Chicago Fire	Tully Monster	Seal

Illinois Bingo

Industry (-ies)	County (-ies)	Crop(s)	Lincoln	James Butler Hickok
Painted Turtle	Monarch Butterfly	Marquette and Joliet	Flag	Flourite
Illinois Territory	Song		Aurora	Shawnee Hills
Gulf Coastal	Seal	Judicial Branch	Prairie	Springfield
Capital	Eastern Tiger Salamander(s)	Tully Monster	Black Hawk	Charles Rudolph Walgreen

Illinois Bingo: Card No. 29

Illinois Bingo

Chicago	Shawnee Hills	Rockford	James Butler Hickok	Springfield
Apple(s)	County (-ies)	Illini	Executive Branch	Aurora
Illinois Territory	Civil War		Flag	Marquette and Joliet
Tully Monster	Black Hawk	Big Bluestem	Prairie	Song
Seal	White Oak	Charles Rudolph Walgreen	Industry (-ies)	Flourite